The Battle

of

Neville's Cross

The Whole Story

by

Simon Webb

Published by the Langley Press, Durham, 2017

The cover includes a detail of a painting by William Duggan:

w.duggan399@gmail.com

Also from the Langley Press

The Prince Bishops of Durham
The Lambton Worm
Mary Ann Cotton: Victorian Serial Killer
In Search of the Little Count
Victorian Durham
In Search of the Northern Saints
The Legend of Saint Cuthbert
In Search of Bede

For free downloads and more from the Langley Press,
visit our website at:
http://tinyurl.com/lpdirect

CONTENTS

When all her chivalry hath been in France
And she a mourning widow of her nobles,
She hath herself not only well defended
But taken and impounded as a stray
The King of Scots; whom she did send to France,
To fill King Edward's fame with prisoner kings
And make her chronicle as rich with praise
As is the ooze and bottom of the sea
With sunken wreck and sunless treasuries.

(The archbishop of Canterbury, from Shakespeare's *Henry V*, Act 1, Scene 2. 'She' is England)

I. In Durham Cathedral

Generations of visitors to Durham have been puzzled by the sorry state of two of the chest-tombs in the south aisle of the city's celebrated cathedral.

These are the resting-places of a father and son, Ralph and John Neville, who both died during the second half of the fourteenth century. They lie with their respective wives in tombs of a type familiar to haunters of old English churches and cathedrals; a type of tomb celebrated by the poet Philip Larkin in his 1964 poem *An Arundel Tomb*.

The bones of Ralph and Alice, and John and Maud Neville, lie in what must have started out as tall, elaborately-decorated stone boxes, while stone effigies of them recline on the lids. But unlike the fourteenth-century tomb in Chichester cathedral that Larkin describes with such delicacy, the Neville tombs at Durham have suffered terrible damage. The effigies of John and Ralph have been reduced to mere torsos scrawled over with incised graffiti, their heads and limbs quite gone. Alice, Ralph's wife, has suffered a similar fate, while Maud is in a slightly better condition than the other three, though her head has been pounded almost flat.

At one time, there must have been a decorative frieze of reliefs around John and Maud's stone box or chest, but this is now quite gone. The frieze around Ralph and Alice's tomb is still present, but the miniature statues that form part of the decoration have all lost their heads, and some of the figures have been lost altogether.

By contrast, the Chichester tomb Larkin described is largely intact: the stone effigies of Richard FitzAlan and his wife Eleanor, contemporaries of Ralph and John Neville, have lifelike, expressive faces, and their fine costumes are rendered in exquisite detail. They rest their heads on stone pillows, and they warm their feet on a lion (for him) and a dog (for her).

What, then, caused the sorry mutilation of the Durham tombs?

It seems that the damage was done by Scottish prisoners of war incarcerated in Durham cathedral over two and a half centuries after John Neville died in 1388. Hundreds of these prisoners, captured after Oliver Cromwell won the Battle of Dunbar in 1650, were locked up here. They tried to keep warm by burning nearly all the woodwork in the cathedral, and can hardly be blamed for taking out their frustrations on the Nevilles. They managed to identify the occupants of the tombs, and remembered that both Ralph and John had fought against the Scots in a memorable battle near Durham on the seventeenth of October 1346: the day all hell broke loose in what are now green fields at the edge of the city.

II. Who Started It?

In tracing the causes of the Battle of Neville's Cross it is possible to go right back to the invasion of England by the Norman, William the Conqueror, in 1066, nearly three hundred years before Ralph and John Neville and their brothers-in-arms faced the Scots at Neville's Cross.

The Norman Conquest left England with a French royal family, and many French aristocrats. Many of these possessed land and other assets across the English Channel, and had no intention of giving them up to concentrate exclusively on their newly-acquired property in England. The cross-Channel interests of the English monarchy were reinforced by the accession of King Henry II to the English throne in 1154. Henry, the first of England's Angevin kings, (meaning that he was the count of Anjou in France) was also duke of Normandy (as William the Conqueror had been) and of

Aquitaine, among other titles. Many English monarchs who came after William and Henry spent a lot of time and money, and caused the deaths of many of their subjects, trying to gain or regain parts of France. Edward III, king of England at the time of the Battle of Neville's Cross, went so far as to claim all the lands the French king ruled, and was even proclaimed king of France in 1340, in an elaborate ceremony in what is now the Belgian city of Ghent.

Two years earlier, in September 1338, Edward had featured in another ceremony, conducted by the German emperor at Coblenz, at which Emperor Louis had declared the English king 'Vicar-General of the Empire in all the Germanies and in all the Almaines'. At that time, Louis also promised to support Edward against Philip VI, the king of France, for seven years.

These spectacular and costly ceremonies were part of Edward's aforementioned plan to gain territory in France, a plan which had many military, political, economic and diplomatic aspects to it. The plan was also saddled with so much complexity and long-windedness, and suffered so many setbacks and adjustments, that a description of it could easily fill a much longer book than this one. Perhaps the most famous

13

military engagement of Edward's campaigns in France was the Battle of Crécy, which the English side, commanded by their king, won, just fifty-two days before the Battle of Neville's Cross was fought, near Durham, in Edward's absence. By the time Edward's brother-in-law David II, king of Scotland, faced Ralph Neville and his comrades on a moor to the west of Durham, the English king was besieging the important French coastal town of Calais.

Although King David of Scotland was married to Edward's sister Joan, there was no love lost between the two kings. Edward was so vexed with the Scots at the time of David's wedding that he refused to attend the service, even though his own sister was the bride. The English king was in his mid-thirties at the time of the Battle of Neville's Cross, but he had been participating in wars against the Scots since his mid-teens. A formal peace had been agreed between the two countries in 1328, but by 1333 Edward was supporting Edward Balliol, a rival king of Scotland who had invaded that country the year before.

King David, who was born a dozen years after Edward, had been an infant king in the year of Balliol's invasion, and by the time of the Battle of Neville's Cross he had had plenty of time to cultivate his resentment concerning the invasion, the coronation of Balliol as a rival king at Scone in 1332, and the years of war that followed.

Balliol ruled Scotland as a puppet of Edward III, and David was forced into exile in France from 1334-1341, while the power of the invader was still strong. King Philip VI of France welcomed David and his queen very kindly, giving them refuge in a château in Normandy, and paying them a pension. David must have remembered Philip's hospitality and support when the French king contacted him after the Battle of Crécy in 1346. Since so many English were away fighting in France, Philip suggested, a Scottish invasion might encounter little resistance, and would also cause discomfort to the English, who were making so such trouble for the French allies of Scotland.

The long-distance French involvement in the 1346 Scottish invasion of England is a reminder that this was an outlying conflict in what nineteenth-century historians came to call the Hundred Years War; a disastrously prolonged conflict between England and France, that also dragged in other nations (like the Scots) and actually lasted for a hundred and sixteen years, from 1337 to 1453. This war thus 'officially' began during the reign of David II's English rival Edward III, and ended during the long and troubled reign of Henry VI (ruled 1422-61).

As well as a sense of loyalty to his allies the French, and lingering resentment against the English, David's invasion was almost certainly motivated by a desire for plunder, a taste for mayhem, and perhaps the wish to appear a strong, warlike king like his father, King Robert I of Scotland, known as Robert the Bruce. The Bruce it was who asserted Scottish independence, won the celebrated battle of Bannockburn (fought against the English in 1314) and has endured as an icon of Scottish boldness and defiance.

Whereas David was probably trying to live up to the legend of his famous father, the English king Edward III was perhaps trying to live down the reputation of his own father, Edward II, regarded by his contemporaries as a weak and ineffectual king. This earlier Edward had been deposed, imprisoned and probably assassinated on the orders of his own wife, Queen Isabella, and her lover, Roger Mortimer. This notorious pair ruled for a time through the infant King Edward III, but when Edward was nearly eighteen years old (in October 1330) he had Mortimer arrested at Nottingham, and later executed without trial at Tyburn in London.

Modern historians are concerned to get at the facts of events such as the 1346 Scottish invasion of England, but many of the chroniclers who wrote about King David's progress were concerned less with the truth, and an even-handed approach, than with glorifying the deeds of those on one side of the conflict, while pouring scorn on the opposition.

Unfortunately these accounts, which can include both fanciful and sarcastic elements, are our main sources for the Battle of Neville's Cross: there were no modern historians in Durham at the time. It is possible to put these accounts together to get a more complete view of what happened, which is what several writers have attempted, but the end result can never be really comprehensive or consistent. A.H. Burne, in his 1952 book *More Battlefields of England*, carefully combined knowledge of medieval warfare and the historical sources with a personal survey of the probable field of battle, together with something called Inherent Military Probability (or I.M.P.); but even his recreation is inconsistent with what may be reliable aspects of at least one of the earliest sources.

Bias is not the only problem with the earliest accounts of the Battle of Neville's Cross. In an age of widespread illiteracy, men in holy orders dominated the fourteenth-century intelligentsia, which means that the chronicles of the time tended to be written by monks. These men may not have had any military experience or training, and may not have been able to grasp even the primitive strategy and tactics behind the wars and battles of their time.

The chronicles of Froissart, Lanercost and Andrew of Wyntoun, which are important sources for events in 1346, include the Battle of Neville's Cross as part of much longer narratives: their accounts of this specific battle might have been more detailed and accurate if they had set out to write only about the Scottish invasion of England of 1346. In the case of the French chronicler Jean Froissart, it is possible that his understanding of the battle became confused in his own mind with an earlier battle or skirmish further north, so that he places the battle of the seventeenth of October 1346 sixty miles away from where it is thought to have happened.

The Chronicle of Lanercost priory in Cumbria is so rabidly anti-Scottish that some of its content would count as offensive to some readers. It insists on calling David 'David the defecator', a reference to an unfortunate accident that occurred while the future king of Scotland was being baptised. The chronicle goes on to call the man that grew from this baby 'a stem of evil' sprung from 'the root of iniquity in Scotland', a stem which, moreover, bore 'buds, root and foliage of much confusion'. The followers of David on his 1346 campaign were 'the sons of iniquity' and 'children of accursed Belial' who dared 'to raise war against God's people, to set sword upon the land, and to ruin peace', 'impelled by pride and led by the devil'.

There is some doubt about the size of David's invasion force, but Lanercost, despite its extreme anti-Scottish bias, is regarded as one of the more reliable sources on these events, and its monkish author asserts that the invader brought more that thirty-two thousand combatants with him. Lanercost itemises these, saying that the lion's share, twenty thousand, were 'hobblers', meaning infantry who rode to the battlefield, but left their horses behind when they actually fought. As well as 'earls, barons, knights and esquires' there were also ten thousand or more foot-soldiers and archers, and two thousand men-at-arms; cavalrymen who were knights in all but name and social rank, who would also fight on foot.

Before David even reached his country's border with England, his force had been reduced by an unfortunate incident, which some took as a bad omen for the rest of the campaign. Among the Scottish magnates who had assembled at the nunnery of Elcho on the banks of the river Tay were William, the earl of Ross, and Ranald, who bore the picturesque title of Lord of the Isles. According to the French chronicler Jean Froissart, Ranald brought with him 'three thousand of the wildest of his countrymen'.

Unfortunately, the earl of Ross and the lord of the isles quarrelled at Elcho, and William killed Ranald. The earl then deserted King David's army, with all his followers.

Lanercost tells us that after entering England 'with a lion-like rush' David's somewhat reduced forces set about besieging the Castle of Liddell, now a ruin in the Scottish border county of Roxburgh. After several days, the siege languished in a stalemate, and the invaders tried the idea, well-worn at the time, of filling in the ditches around the castle with stones, earth, wood and brushwood, then directly accessing the walls, with their shields over their heads to protect them from whatever the occupants rained down on them.

Some besieging armies used special 'penthouses' or portable shelters when they were breaking into a castle in this way, but, using just their shields for protection, the Scots were able to break a hole in the wall: once inside they 'killed all whom they found, with few exceptions' (probably women and children) including 'the governor of the fortress', Sir Walter de Selby.

Selby pleaded with King David to spare him, saying that he wanted to die in battle, like a true knight. 'Oh fearful king,' he pleaded, 'if you truly want to act like a king, surely you can allow me some drops from the fountain of your grace?' But his pleading was to no avail: he was summarily beheaded, before he could even make a confession.

Lanercost puts pitiful pleas into Selby's mouth to encourage the reader to deplore his murder, but in fact the master of Liddell was not exactly an innocent lamb led to the slaughter. In September 1317 Selby had been a leading member of a party of robbers who had attached Louis Beaumont, then the new bishop of Durham, as he entered his bishopric. The other victims of these medieval highwaymen included two cardinals and the new bishop's brother, Henry de Beaumont. Not content with stealing the travellers' valuables, the robbers kidnapped the bishop and forced him to pay a ransom for his own release.

After Liddell Castle, the Scots wrecked Lanercost Priory itself, which may explain much of the bitterness the chronicler felt towards these unwelcome visitors from the northern kingdom.

At Lanercost 'they entered arrogantly into the sanctuary, threw out the vessels of the temple, plundered the treasury, shattered the bones [presumably relics of saints and martyrs], stole the jewels, and destroyed as much as they could'.

After bypassing Carlisle, the invaders went on to wreck another priory, at Hexham, though they did not destroy Hexham itself. Likewise David 'strictly ordered' that Corbridge, Darlington and Durham City 'should not be burnt' because he intended to ransack these places for supplies, should he remain in the north of England throughout the winter.

On the night before he entered what we call County Durham, which was then known as the Bishopric of Durham, King David was warned in a dream not to enter this country at all, since it was under the protection of St Cuthbert, the seventh-century monk whose remains still lie in Durham cathedral.

Shaking off his dream, and arriving near the city of Durham, the Scottish king made a temporary headquarters at the manor of Beaurepaire, near the modern village of Bearpark, to the west of the city. Here David boasted that he would soon see London: this turned out to be a true prophecy, but it did not come to pass in the way he hoped.

The first buildings of the manor of Beaurepaire had been put up by Prior Bertram de Middleton of Durham as a retirement home for himself in 1258. These were extended in later centuries, and the ruins of some of the buildings still survive, by a bend in the river Browney, to the north-east of modern Bearpark.

Beaurepaire or Old Bearpark was used by David as a base for raiding parties that, according to Lanercost, tried to do as much damage to the surrounding area as they could: burning houses and churches, killing the locals and commandeering supplies.

But further south, the English military response was already in hand: the French king's advice that his ally the king of Scotland would meet with little resistance in England soon turned out to be very bad advice indeed.

III. Who Was Who

Looking back on the fourteenth century from the perspective of the twenty-first, it is possible to see many negative factors operating that we still have to contend with today. Leaders of countries still invade other countries on the basis of poor intelligence; invading armies still gather plunder, wreck sacred sites and commit atrocities, and wars are still fought because of festering resentment left over from previous wars.

There is also a tendency for countries to go to war in support of their allies, other nations whose interests may not be identical to their own. Greed is still a motivation for war, even if the armies involved do not indulge in looting; though the greed for land that inspired King David is a little alien to us. The tendency for innocent civilians, including women, elderly people, and children to suffer as a result of war is actually more of a feature of war today than it was in the Middle Ages.

Although modern nations profess peace, war is still used by the leaders of nations to convince potential critics that they are strong and resolute. One justification for war, the feeling that the enemy are evil, dangerous, inferior, degenerate, impious or otherwise deserving of death, is still commonly used today.

Although peace is central to the purest forms of the great world religions, religious leaders still support war, as happened to a remarkable extent in the case of the Battle of Neville's Cross, as we shall see.

Although some aspects of David's over-confident invasion may seem depressingly familiar even from the twenty-first century perspective, some features of life in mid fourteenth-century Britain are so unfamiliar that it is necessary to stand back and pause for a second to take them in.

Perhaps the most bizarre feature of fourteenth-century life in the west of Europe, at least from the perspective of the modern English-speaking world, is the vast power and wealth of the Roman Catholic Church at this time. The worldly Pope Clement VI, who was pontiff in 1346, could serve as a personification of how this ecclesiastical wealth and power could be both used and abused.

Thomas Hatfield, bishop of Durham at the time of the Battle of Neville's Cross, was an obvious protégé of Edward III, acted as a kind of senior civil servant for the king, went on military expeditions both for him and with him, and was the king's candidate for see of Durham in 1345, when he was around thirty-five years old. When some cardinals complained to the pope about Hatfield's election, Clement VI remarked that the monks of Durham would have elected a donkey if the king had hinted that they should do so.

Although Hatfield's election was controversial, he could hardly have been less well-suited to the position of bishop of Durham than Louis Beaumont, the bishop who had been robbed and kidnapped by Walter de Selby and his accomplices in 1317. The Durham chronicler Robert Greystanes claimed that Louis had insufficient Latin to get through his first service in the cathedral, although he had been carefully coached for days beforehand. He also lacked the full range of military skills expected from a bishop or archbishop in those days, as, according to different sources, he was either lame in one or both legs, or had a club foot. King Edward II accused him of negligence and laziness in connection with his duty to help protect the north of England from the Scots. As bishops of Durham had done before him, Louis preferred to pay the Scots money to leave Durham alone, regularly handing them the equivalent of over two hundred thousand pounds at today's values.

Five years before Thomas Hatfield became bishop of Durham, William Zouche had been elected archbishop of York, not because of, but in spite of, King Edward III's opinion on who should fill this ancient role. Zouche, who had served Edward as what we would call a civil servant, a politician, a military leader and even a merchant, had to travel to Avignon to Pope Clement to be confirmed in his post against his monarch's wishes. Since Zouche had had experience of fighting the Scots in the 1330s, it is not surprising that he should have been one of the three men who mustered an army to oppose King David's 1346 invasion. When this army organised itself into three divisions before the Battle of Neville's Cross, it was therefore the archbishop of York who took command of the centre division, facing the king of Scotland and his own centre division. Lanercost tells us that the English army put its trust, 'not in swords, helmets, lances, corselets, or other gilded armour, but only in the name of Christ'.

The three leaders of the military response to David's invasion were the archbishop, Ralph Neville (whom we have already met) and Henry Percy.

As the ruined magnificence of his tomb in Durham cathedral would seem to suggest, Neville was a man of considerable wealth. His power and the strength of his reputation is confirmed by the mere presence of his tomb in the cathedral: he was the first layman to be granted such an honour. In his mid-fifties at the time of the Battle of Neville's Cross, Ralph had been fighting for Edward II and Edward III against the Scots since at least his twenties; as his father had fought for Edward I and Edward II.

Ralph was only a second son, but his older brother Robert had been killed by the Scots in 1318, which allowed him to inherit.

Henry Percy, second lord Percy, was some ten years younger than Ralph Neville, but by the time of the Battle of Neville's Cross he had already been fighting the Scots for nearly a quarter of a century. Percy was one of the 'disinherited': Englishmen and Scotsmen who had lost land in Scotland due to the success of Robert the Bruce's campaign to make that country independent. In 1326 Percy managed to get back the lands he claimed in Galloway and

Angus by peaceful means, during negotiations with the Bruce. But in 1333 Percy saw Edward Balliol's invasion of Scotland as an opportunity to gain more lands, and he joined Balliol and other disinherited men, on the promise of lands that would bring him an additional income of two thousand marks per year.

Although the triumvirate of York, Percy and Neville are usually named as the leaders of the English at Neville's Cross, one of the three English divisions was led by Thomas Rokeby, another veteran of many battles against the Scots, who was probably in his mid-forties in 1346. One of the perennial problems of warfare in those days before radios, reconnaissance aircraft and satellite intel, was actually finding the enemy. It seems that in 1327 Edward III became so frustrated by this that he offered a hundred pounds a year to anyone who could bring him within sight of the Scots. The prize, worth well over thirty thousand a year today, was won by Rokeby.

The English commanders at Neville's Cross were certainly experienced – the four described above were on average twenty years older than the men who led each of the three Scottish divisions in the battle. The contrast in age and experience looks starkest when we compare Ralph Neville and the Scottish king, David II.

Ralph was probably around fifty-five at the time of the battle, whereas David was twenty-two or twenty-three.

As well as being experienced, the English leaders may also have been pretty well-motivated: they all had interests in the north to protect, and they may have known that if the Scots were beaten back on this occasion, this would give the English an opportunity to gain or regain land in Scotland. If it is true that Edward Balliol, Edward III's candidate for the post of Scottish king, also fought on the English side in the battle, then he personally might have been very well-motivated: for him, Neville's Cross may have looked like the start of another chance to be a monarch.

The men who led the three Scottish divisions in the Battle of Neville's Cross were certainly less experienced than their English equivalents, and it is likely that both William Douglas and Robert Stewart were not as motivated as David, their young leader, would have liked.

According to the Scottish historian John Parker Lawson, writing in 1839, Douglas had counselled David to finish his foray into England after he had taken Liddell Castle, an action that consolidated Douglas's power in this area, but was of less interest to David and the other Scottish barons.

For his own part, Robert Stewart's lack of morale may have gone beyond Douglas's feeling that the Scots should have turned back some days earlier. Indeed it might be argued that Stewart's interests would have been best served by the loss of the battle and even the death of King David II.

Stewart was the grandson of Robert the Bruce, the son of his daughter Marjorie. Since the Bruce had no legitimate sons until 1324, Robert had spent part of his childhood expecting to become king when his grandfather died; but the old man remarried and fathered a son, the future David II, in 1324, when he was fifty. But since King David had had no legitimate children of either sex by the time of the Battle of Neville's Cross, Robert Stewart was still his official heir.

IV. The Battle

It seems that in the case of the Battle of Neville's Cross, it did not take the two armies very long to find each other.

According to Lanercost, the English force, which had assembled at the County Durham town of Barnard Castle, proceeded to Bishop Auckland and 'pitching their tents in a certain beautiful woodland near the aforesaid town, the English army spent the whole night there'. At dawn (around 6:20) the next morning Sir William Douglas rode out from the Scots' headquarters at Bearpark 'with 500 men to harry the country and gather spoil'.

Douglas and his men headed due south about seven miles, and found the village of Merrington (now Kirk Merrington) which they proceeded to plunder. As they were at their work, a thick mist fell over the area, out of which they soon heard the sound of an approaching army. In their panic, the Scots ran right into the English force, which had marched from Bishop Auckland, just under five miles away.

There then followed a skirmish, during which many Scots were killed; followed by a bloodthirsty chase, when a detachment of English riders under Robert Ogle followed at the heels of Douglas's men, killing as many as they could. This action is commemorated in the modern name of a road that lies a couple of miles north of Merrington, to the north-east of Spennymoor: Butcher's Race.

Douglas himself, and around two hundred other Scots who rode armoured horses, escaped Ogle's attentions: Ogle himself eventually had to abandon the chase because his horse became exhausted.

That, at least, is what Lanercost says about this preliminary skirmish. To give an idea of how accounts can differ, the verse chronicle of the Scotsman Andrew of Wyntoun says that Douglas clashed with the English at Ferryhill (which he calls Ferry of the Hill) about two and a half miles to the east. According to Wyntoun, the chase that followed proceeded to 'Swndyrsand' (probably Sunderland Bridge) about three miles to the north, where five hundred Scotsmen were killed 'by dint of hand' (presumably the Scottish chronicler thought that Douglas had set

33

off with rather more than five hundred in the first place).

Back at Bearpark, Douglas burst in on King David, demanding that he get ready because 'The English have attacked us.'

David refused to believe this. 'There are no men in England,' he said, 'but wretched monks, lewd priests, swineherds, cobblers and skinners. They dare not face me: I am safe enough.'

While David and William were arguing in this way, a small group of monks from Durham arrived, hoping to sue for peace. At that time, and until the dissolution of the monasteries, Durham had both a cathedral and a priory all under one roof. Lanercost describes these monks as 'black monks', meaning Benedictines. The Scottish king suspected that the holy brothers, holding their metaphorical olive branch before them, had been sent by the English to distract him while their advancing army surrounded his position. David ordered that the monks be beheaded, but as the Scots got ready for action against the English, they were forgotten and managed to escape back to Durham.

This was not, however, the last David was to see of the Durham monks. It seems that the prior himself, Prior Fossor, had had a dream instructing him to take a party of his brethren, armed with a sacred cloth of St Cuthbert's, to the battlefield itself to pray for mercy. This they did, setting up their prayer meeting at Maiden's Bower, a round cairn to the east of the place where the Scots stood and stared at the English for a while before the battle proper commenced. Later the sacred cloth, called a corporax cloth (used to cover the chalice during mass) was sewn into a victory banner. Later still, this banner was destroyed by Katherine Whittingham, the wife of the first post-dissolution dean of Durham.

Prior Fossor wrote a letter to Thomas Hatfield, the bishop of Durham, describing the battle. From Maiden's Bower, he would not have seen much, at least not until the Scots started to retreat, but he probably would have heard the dreadful sounds of the battle mingling with the prayers, psalms and chants of his party. Meanwhile, another party of monks stood praying and watching from the tower of the cathedral. Fossor's letter is proof that the bishop himself was not present at the battle – he was probably in France at the time.

Although the Scots advanced from a place near Maiden's Bower, where Fossor knelt in prayer, and though the retreating Scots were scattered over the whole area, the monks were not molested, even though the Scots had recently wrecked and terrorised a number of sacred places on their route to Durham. This was seen as a miracle.

In his letter to the bishop, Fossor describes the tragic sight of the dead lying naked on the battlefield, their bodies having been stripped of clothes, armour, helmets, weapons, footwear and valuables by the enemy army and the local inhabitants, in the aftermath of the battle. According to *The Rites of Durham*, a sixteenth-century account of Durham as it was before the Reformation, Prior Fossor, on behalf of the cathedral and St Cuthbert, claimed many 'most excellent jewels and monuments which were brought from Scotland, and other noblemen's banners'. The most precious non-human prize was the so-called 'Black Rood of Scotland', a relic that had belonged to St Margaret, an eleventh-century queen of Scotland, which is supposed to have incorporated a piece of the cross on which Christ was crucified.

According to Andrew of Wyntoun, the Scots 'made them great mirth and solacing' at Bearpark, which suggests that King David at least may have been in bed, hung over or possibly still drunk when Douglas, no doubt breathless, sweating and pale with fright, delivered his news. Since he felt he had nothing to fear from the English, David may have seen no reason to keep himself and his followers ready for action while they were lodged at Bearpark.

Whether it was ready or not, David's force soon found itself facing the archbishop of York's army about a third of a mile north of Neville's Cross.

Today this area at the western edge of Durham City is partly built over with roads, houses, shops, footbridges, gardens and a farm. The Scots may have stood ready for battle in what is now grazing land to the west of the A167. In the fourteenth century, this whole area, part of which is still called Crossgate Moor, was probably rough moorland, of the type that can be seen today in the Durham Dales to the west of the county. According to R.A. Lomas's attempt to reconstruct the landscape as it was then (in Rollason and Prestwich's book *The Battle of Neville's Cross*) this type of moorland would have been characterised by rough grass, furze, heather, and few if any trees.

The two armies stood about five hundred yards apart, both on ridges, with a dry valley between them. Although King David may have refused to let himself accept this, it must have been clear even to a knight peering out through the narrow slits at the front of his helmet that the English army was standing on a better ridge.

Theirs, south-east of the Scots, was broad and fairly flat, whereas the Scots found themselves on a narrower ridge, surrounded by cliffs, bogs, hills and ditches, and perhaps even fences and hay-ricks.

The commanders of both armies must have realised that if they advanced, their troops would eventually be slowed down as they passed through the bottom of the valley that lay between them. Today this area is fenced, and also clogged with bushes and small trees, and it is not inconceivable that a small modern tank could get stuck there.

It is possible that the two armies stood and stared at each other for quite a time. It is not clear how the stalemate was broken, but David Butler, writing twenty years ago in a book intended to mark the six hundred and fiftieth anniversary of the battle, suggested that Sir William Douglas began to advance with his right wing.

As must have seemed inevitable, at least from the English side, Douglas's troops became tangled up in the bottom of the valley, before many of them could even start to climb the steep hill that led to the English position. Worse, the right-hand division of the Scots was now within range of the longbowmen of Sir Thomas Rokeby's left-hand division.

Seeing that the right-hand Scottish division was being cut to pieces, John Graham, earl of Menteith, begged King David to give him a hundred mounted knights, so that he could 'scale', or reduce the numbers of, the deadly English archers. This had worked for the Scots at the Battle of Bannockburn in 1314, but then five hundred horsemen had dispersed Edward II's archers, who had found themselves in a poor position, not properly supported by other troops.

Deciding, perhaps, that Neville's Cross could be no Bannockburn, and that the enemy archers were in too strong a position, King David refused Graham his hundred knights. But the earl could not be restrained, and conducted a cavalry charge of his own, or with a small contingent of his own men.

Amazingly, the Graham survived his reckless charge, but his horse was killed. According to Charles Oman's classic study of medieval warfare, this sort of 'loose cannon' behaviour was fairly common among the mounted knights and higher aristocrats of the armies of the Hundred Years War. Describing the French army, Oman writes that its upper echelon 'was composed of a fiery and undisciplined aristocracy, which imagined itself to be the most efficient military force in the world, but was in reality little removed from an armed mob'.

Although he survived his own reckless charge, Menteith's participation in the Battle of Neville's Cross proved disastrous to him in the end. While his monarch was merely imprisoned in London and elsewhere, the Graham's severed head was exhibited on a stake in the English capital.

As the men of Douglas's division on the Scottish right were still being helplessly slaughtered, the Scottish centre and left 'battles', under King David and Robert Stewart respectively, were better able to advance on the English, as they had easier terrain to cover.

While English armies of this period were relying increasingly on their archers, the Scots trusted to their 'schiltrons', an old Anglo-Saxon word that they applied to bodies of pikemen. These infantrymen wielded pikes – in effect, sturdy spears that were too long and heavy to throw, and had to be used with two hands. These could be very effective against both infantry and cavalry, but were useless if the schiltrons couldn't get close enough to the enemy to use them. And it was part of the job of the archers to stop too many advancing pikemen getting too close.

Presumably, the Scots centre and left battles at Neville's Cross managed to advance quickly enough to get to the English archers before too many of them had been downed with arrows. In any case, it seems that the most northerly sections of both armies found themselves fighting hand-to-hand.

Their archers gave the English a deadly advantage at the start of the battle, and their reserve force of cavalry, which is supposed to have been under the command of Edward Balliol, turned the battle into an English victory.

The reserve horsemen had been waiting in the rear of the English force, possibly quite near Neville's Cross itself. Soon the Scots found themselves with fresh English cavalry to their left, their right division hopelessly crippled, and with the English centre encircling the Scots centre, and threatening King David himself. It was now that Robert Stewart decided that this might be a good time to make an exit, though whether he left alone, or with a small detachment of his closest followers, or with a more substantial part of his division, is unclear.

Stewart's flight, and that of Patrick, the ninth earl of Dunbar, was used by the Lanercost chronicler as an excuse to deploy more of his characteristic sarcasm. After asserting that Patrick resembled a priest in his reluctance to fight, Lanercost says:

Overcome by cowardice, [Stewart] broke his vow to God that he would never await the first blow in battle. He flies with the priest, and as a good cleric, will assist the mass to be celebrated by the other. These two, turning their backs, fought with great success, for they entered Scotland with their division and without a single wound; and so they led off the dance, leaving David to dance as he felt inclined.

Note that Lanercost implies that Stewart took his whole division with him. The reference to dancing at the end of the passage above is in line with Lanercost's other references to King David of Scotland as the namesake of the Biblical King David, the father of Solomon, who 'danced before Yahweh with all his might' (2 Samuel 6:14). Of course the Scottish David comes off worst when Lanercost compares him to that earlier David.

The final stage of the Battle of Neville's Cross saw King David's centre division surrounded by the English. The Scots are supposed to have defended their young king until there were only eighty of them left: by now the rest were either dead, injured or running away, most of the fliers probably heading north-west, back to Bearpark.

David was either captured right there on the field of battle or, as the legend goes, he fled alone, badly injured, and hid under Aldin Grange Bridge, a narrow crossing over the River Browney. There his reflection in the water was spotted by one John Copeland, who may have been riding up and down the area of the Scots' retreat trying to find a high-status Scotsman to capture: such a prize might have made his fortune, since the family of his captive might have been prepared to pay a large ransom. When Copeland realised that he'd found the king of Scotland, he must have felt that he'd hit the jackpot.

King David didn't come quietly: he is supposed to have whacked Copeland with one of his armoured gauntlets, giving his captor a gash on his face, and depriving him of two or more of his teeth. But Copeland held on to his prize, refusing to give him up until he had reached King Edward III at Calais. There he was awarded a pension of five hundred pounds a year, equivalent to over two hundred thousand today. According to J.W. Dickenson, writing in 1991 about the aftermath of the battle, Copeland had been a border reiver, little more than a brigand or land-pirate of the north country; but his efforts at Neville's Cross earned him a pardon along with his new-found wealth. He bought Crook Hall near Durham, part of the structure of which remains more or less as he would have known it.

King David was not the only aristocratic Scotsman captured after the battle. *The Rites of Durham* tells us that the prisoners also included four Scottish earls, two lords, a bishop, and an archbishop, among others.

Also according to *The Rites of Durham*, fifteen thousand Scotsmen had been killed in the battle, including 'seven earls' and 'many lords'.

V. Aftermath

The sources disagree on the nature and extent of the wounds King David sustained at the Battle of Neville's Cross. If we put the different accounts together and opt for the 'maximum' option, then by the time of his capture he had two arrows lodged in his head, of which one or more may have been in his face, and one arrow in his leg.

Because the arrows used with the English or Welsh longbow were barbed, the classic way to remove them with minimal additional injury was to push them right through, carefully avoiding major organs and blood-vessels if possible. Where the arrow was longed against bone, as in the case of a facial injury, pushing the thing right through was not an option.

The future English king Henry V had an arrow-head lodged in his face after the Battle of Shrewsbury in 1403. This was removed by carefully widening the wound itself, extracting the arrow-head and treating the now 'empty' wound with honey, turpentine and a barley poultice. Presumably some such procedure was used on the captive Scottish king. The arrow-head lodged in his leg is said to have popped out spontaneously while he was praying. This was either a miracle, or a case of the body rejecting a foreign object that it did not recognise as part of itself.

Although his physical wounds from the Battle of Neville's Cross healed perhaps better than anyone living before the time of modern antiseptics and antibiotics had a right to expect, the young king's psychological trauma must have been harder to cope with. In planning and executing his 1346 invasion of England he had miscalculated badly: he might also have been misled by King Phillip of France, who may not have had very good information about the strength of the English forces in the north of England in the first place. The disastrous outcome of the battle (for the Scots) was proof that Edward III's allies in the north could match and overcome even a very large force of Scottish invaders.

Subsequent events would show, however, that Edward's commitments in France made it impossible for him to follow up the English army's victory near Durham by overrunning the whole of Scotland. The Battle of Neville's Cross happened in October 1346, but it was not until six months later that a small English force led by Edward Balliol set out from Carlisle, ostensibly to win back Scotland from the Scots. Demoralised and kingless, it seems that the Scots paid the English the equivalent of around four million pounds in modern money to make a truce. The castles of Edinburgh, Stirling and Dunbar were still in Scottish hands, but large areas of Scotland south of the Clyde and the Forth were now controlled by the English.

With their young king now a prisoner in England, relations between the Scots and the English became less the concern of soldiers than that of what we would now call diplomats, politicians, negotiators and accountants. At Berwick in 1357, eleven years after the battle where he had been captured, King David accepted the terms of a treaty whereby he would be returned to his kingdom in exchange for a ransom equivalent to over two million pounds in modern money, payable in ten annual instalments. The Scots soon defaulted on these payments, and in fact Edward III was never paid in full. Much of the debt was written off in 1369, when a fourteen-year truce was agreed.

The Battle of Neville's Cross is now remembered as one where the tide of the fighting was turned because of the contribution of the English archers. The English or Welsh longbow, the characteristic weapon of the deadliest of these archers, may have had a range of up to four hundred yards; the length of about fifteen tennis-courts. Famously, the arrows could penetrate the chain-mail and leather armour worn during the early phases of the Hundred Years' War; though when plate-armour became more widespread, the usefulness of the longbow was diminished.

In battle, the bowmen, who might start with as many as seventy arrows each, would stick their arrows upright in the ground at their feet, and shoot at a rate of as many as six arrows a minute. Unlike modern soldiers, who might have no military skills at all at the time of their recruitment, many of the English longbowmen would have practised archery from boyhood: in fact Edward III tried to enforce laws obliging all fit men and boys to do so regularly, and even to refrain from other sports.

Thanks to constant practice, medieval longbowmen could use bows that it took almost superhuman strength to draw. Examination of the skeletons of archers from the period has revealed that their bones changed under the repeated stress. They even developed bone spurs, painful outgrowths on wrists, shoulders and fingers.

Despite the key role the longbowmen played in the Battle of Neville's Cross, the chronicles of Lanercost, Froissart and Wyntoun barely mention archers. This is probably because, from the chroniclers' point of view, battles were fought by aristocratic, and even royal, knights. In fact, as Charles Oman asserts, the magnificently accoutred knights who turned out at Neville's Cross, and the masses of pikemen who supported them, had been rendered pretty much obsolete by the longbow for nearly fifty years, since the Battle of Falkirk in 1298. This battle was fought between armies led by the English king Edward I and the Scottish rebel leader William Wallace, the hero of the 1995 film *Braveheart*. The battle has a Durham connection, since an important cavalry charge was led by the then bishop of Durham, Antony Bek.

VI. Remembrance

The fact that there were hundreds of Scottish prisoners incarcerated in Durham Cathedral in 1650 reflects the fact that the Battle of Neville's Cross did not mark an end to Anglo-Scottish wars. In fact the two nations would continue to fight for nearly another century after the Battle of Dunbar – until after the Battle of Culloden in 1746. The wars continued despite the fact that a Scottish king, James I, had been crowned king of England in 1603, and despite the Acts of Union of 1706 and 1707.

The imprisonment in Durham cathedral of hundreds of captives taken after the Civil War Battle of Dunbar in 1650 is one of the darkest passages in the history of the cathedral itself. A plaque in the cathedral, that commemorates what the Scots call the Dunbar Martyrs, admits that 'many hundreds died during their imprisonment'. Most died of starvation, because the food that had been provided for them was not actually supplied to them. Among these hundreds of dead were boys as young as thirteen. A number of skeletons of these seventeenth-century Scotsmen were recently unearthed during building work on Palace Green, in front of the cathedral: proof, if proof were needed, that in a place like Durham, if you scratch the skin of the city, history will bleed through.

The probable site of the Battle of Neville's Cross is marked today by information boards set up on the six hundred and fiftieth anniversary of the battle in 1996, and by the cross at Neville's Cross itself. The board attached to the railings that now surround this structure includes a picture of what the cross might have looked like centuries ago, but points out that there is little or nothing of the original cross remaining. Although Ralph Neville may have ordered the erection of an elaborate stone cross, to commemorate the battle, it is likely that there was already a wayside cross here years before the battle itself.

Whatever the origins and history of the cross that stood here until long after the Reformation, it seems that by 1589 the cross, which seems to have incorporated statues of the four Evangelists, together with a stone crucifix, was looking a little too Roman Catholic. It was in that year that it 'was broken down and defaced by some lewd and wicked persons'.

According to *The Rites of Durham* there was once another cross, 'a beautiful cross of wood . . . finely wrought, very large, and of two yards height' which stood on the site of the Maiden's Bower, where Prior Fossor and his party prayed for an English victory. Like the stone cross at Neville's Cross, this was also 'defaced, and thrown down, by some lewd and ill-disposed persons, who despised the antiquity and worthiness of monuments, after the suppression of the abbeys'.

Sources

Introduction to the Sources

Although several contemporary or near-contemporary accounts of the battle have been preserved, these contradict each other; and even when they are combined together, they do not give a very detailed picture of what happened. As a result, we cannot say with any certainty how many combatants were involved, which leaders were definitely present, exactly where the battle happened, when it started, how long it lasted or how many were killed or injured.

We are left in the dark, or at least in a mist, about these details because surviving accounts of the battle, though fairly numerous, are generally short, and tend to be written from a particular political, religious or national point of view. The account from the Chronicle of Lanercost printed below is fairly detailed, and is particularly good on the early days of David's invasion, but it comes from a monastery that was frequently raided by the Scots, and the account is consequently vehemently anti-Scottish. The Lanercost account also spends a lot of time drawing comparisons between various characters in the story and their equivalents in the Old Testament or the Biblical Apocrypha. By contrast, the account from the verse chronicle of the Scottish monk Andrew of Wyntoun tries to play down the extent of the Scots' humiliation by 'bigging up' the numbers of the English force, and shrinking down the numbers of Scots combatants to a mere two thousand.

The treatment of the battle in the sixteenth-century *Rites of Durham* is mainly concerned with the aftermath of the battle and how it affected the city's celebrated cathedral; whereas Prior Fossor's letter to Bishop Hatfield tries to reassure the bishop that the Scottish menace has indeed been batted away, at least for now, though it is also truthful about some of the alarming consequences of the invasion.

In any case, there is no reliable, unbiased contemporary or near-contemporary account of the battle extant. That of the Frenchman Jean Froissart, in his own chronicle, might be expected to be well-balanced, since the chronicler had both English and French connections, but unfortunately Froissart seems to have confused the battle with another engagement that happened further north, and he also introduces the queen of England into the action, when it is very unlikely that she was there.

Unreliable as they may be, the texts printed below are, however, some of our only direct, specific sources of information on the Battle of Neville's Cross; and they reveal more than just fragments of information on the battle. They reflect the attitudes of their age (particularly its religious outlook) and a very medieval approach to history – as a source of messages from the past, to be applied to the present, about the characteristics of certain peoples, the motivations behind certain actions, and the way that right and wrong, wisdom and folly, might be seen to have been rewarded and punished in the aftermath of certain events.

Monk though he undoubtedly was, the Scottish author Andrew of Wyntoun was not enough of a dogmatic Christian to insist that virtue and innocence would always be rewarded in just measure by the special karma meted out by the Christian God. He invokes another sort of deity when he is trying to explain the Scottish defeat:

[Fortune] should not, therefore, be reproved for

being false or treacherous, or for overturning things, since it is in her nature to be forever changing; winning people's trust with her gifts, great or small, and making fools believe that she will always be generous.

I. An Eyewitness Account

The translation printed below is from a draft of a letter, written in Latin, from the prior and convent of Durham to Thomas Hatfield, Bishop of Durham. The Latin text is printed in a book called Historical Papers and Letters from the Northern Registers, *edited by James Raine, which was published by Longman in 1873.*

The letter is supposed to have been written by Prior Fossor of Durham, the master of the monastic community there, which lived cheek by jowl with the city's cathedral and the powerful bishop of Durham.

As is described in section III below, Prior Fossor had a dream before the battle, and felt obliged to go out to a site very near the battle-field, accompanied by a party of monks, to pray for an English victory. Perhaps out of modesty, Fossor doesn't mention this brave action in his letter to Bishop Hatfield.

It is thought that the prior would not have seen the battle from Maiden's Bower, where he is said to have set up his prayer-meeting, but he would probably have heard it, and seen the Scots fleeing from the battle when an English victory seemed assured. What Fossor did see were the stripped bodies of the dead soldiers.

Fossor implies that the Scots heavily outnumbered the English, and this conflicts with other sources. It was common bias to suggest such disparities, but had Fossor been closer to the action he might have supplied much more precise detail than we have here on the two sides and their dispositions. There is a telling absence of precise detail about the fighting, and King David's wound has a generic sound about it.

Fossor follows common practice in writing with some bias: his suggestion that the Scots killed innocent locals before the battle is predictably different to the Scottish version of their behaviour. The suggestion that very much larger numbers of Scots died is not necessarily unreliable. The English archers supplied the crucial advantage, as at Crécy in France, just days before.

The fact that Fossor found it necessary to describe the battle to the bishop is taken as evidence that Hatfield himself was not present, though the French chronicler Jean Froissart insists that he was. It is likely that the bishop was in France, fighting alongside the English king Edward III at this time.

Fossor's Latin is clear and concise: only his florid gratitude to the Almighty might jar somewhat with modern tastes. It is frustrating but unsurprising that the prior is silent on so many details which would interest us. One sentence alone (on Hayden Hall) seems to have suffered some grammatical loss or confusion during the transmission of the text. His concluding piece of aetiology on the derivation of Findon Hill manages to segue between English, Latin and French with a concluding note of reverence. The Bishop would have been impressed.

A Letter Addressed to the Bishop about the Battle of Neville's Cross

Reverend Father,

I am sure that your Reverence will already have received various letters from different people about the cruel atrocities committed by Scottish tribes on English soil, but I wanted to add to your delight over what has happened by passing on what I know of these events; so I am conveying an eye-witness account for your Lordship's attention, and hope it will reassure you.

Shortly after the Feast of Saint Michael the Archangel, the above-mentioned Scots, in a febrile state, invaded English territory with a combined force of knights and foot-soldiers which, according to later reports on the same subject, they considered too strong for the combined resistance of France and England. They utterly destroyed the territory they crossed and surrounding areas with arson and murder, showing scant regard for women, the aged or children. And among the atrocities they committed of this kind, they seized a fortified building under the guardianship of W. de Selby; anyone they found there, they killed. After that they occupied another fortified manor, called Hayden Hall, near Corbridge, which surrendered to them in exchange for the lives of its people.

Their next move was a series of forced marches which brought them on the fateful day in October at about mid-day to a position close to the city of Durham, above the moor of Beaurepaire; there they displayed themselves in dressed ranks as if there was a concerted battle plan. Then suddenly, without further delay, they wheeled towards our manor of Beaurepaire where they camped all that night, within the park's boundary, leaving no-one isolated outside, as I could verify beyond any doubt.

The venerable father, his Grace the Archbishop of York and other nobles who accompanied him – I am sure you can discover their particular identities from other sources more reliably than from me – concealed themselves that same night on your property at Auckland Park.

Then the following day – that would have been the seventeenth of October – our forces deployed themselves on the approaches to Beaurepaire Moor which I mentioned earlier, while the Scots, now aware of their movements, lined themselves up for battle on the high ground above the moor, adjacent to the park; there was then a stand-off between nine o'clock and noon between the two armies. Their standards were visible between the town of Durham and Beaurepaire and the two armies closed to within a short distance of each other.

Thereupon, at the named hour – noon – in what can only add to the delight of our English Church body – the two sides fought a hard, bitter and remorseless battle. But – blessed be Almighty God, in Whose hand lie the very lives of our kings, as it pleases Him to wound and heal, to throw man down and raise him up – the English defeated the Scots in a marvellous triumph, and the natives of our northern lands, whom the Scots had tyrannised for years, have been restored to the enjoyment of that freedom they so desire. David, self-styled 'king of Scotland', was seriously wounded in the battle, and captured: he was struck by an arrow in the face. In fact there were heavy casualties among the braver men from all over Scotland, and those who lie on Beaurepair Moor have been shockingly stripped of their clothes and possessions.

I cannot give you precise numbers of the dead. Others, I am sure, can do so. There were plenty of prisoners of course; perhaps the most notorious – I do not say the bravest – is William Douglas. I am providing a list for you of their names in the enclosed schedule. We lost a few men in the battle too. The site of the battle which concluded the war was between the town of Durham and a certain hill named 'Findon'. Indeed the hill is reputed to have acquired its name from some foreboding of this battle, when its name of Findon was thought to imply some significance for future events: the hill would 'provide a conclusion' or 'fin-don', as it were. For the name is widely understood to refer to the conclusion – or 'fin' to this wretched altercation between English and Scots, which has strengthened over many generations, and has now been concluded by the intervention of He whose powers know no such bounds, or 'fin'.

Translated by William Duggan, 2015.

II. A Scottish Point of View

From the Verse Chronicle of Andrew of Wyntoun, c. 1350 – c. 1425; Book VIII, Chapter XL, Lines 6063-6281.

Andrew of Wyntoun was the prior of an Augustinian monastic community based on St Serf's Inch, an island in Loch Leven in central Scotland, about twenty miles north of Edinburgh. His verse chronicle, written in the English of the Scots of his time, is nothing less than an attempt to versify the whole history of the world, with a special emphasis on Scotland. The chronicle continues after its account of the Battle of Neville's Cross, and stretches to events that occurred around 1420. Note that Wyntoun was probably born a few years after the battle: he relied on other writers for much of his material, and some of his sources may now be lost.

The translation below, based on David Laing's 1872 edition of the chronicle, is prefaced by a short extract from the beginning of Wyntoun's original verse treatment of what he calls the Battle of Durham.

Although Wyntoun's poem is of great historical interest, few readers have been impressed with his skill as a poet, though his verse has a kind of raw vigour, and there are touches of real humour in places. Writing about the Battle of Neville's Cross, Wyntoun has the problem of trying to incorporate an account of what was a disastrous defeat for the Scots into a patriotic chronicle. Although he implies that King David II was a fool, since only 'fools believe that [Fortune] will always be generous', by the time he begins to tackle the subject of Fortune, he has already reminded us that David was very young.

Wyntoun reduces the humiliation of the defeat for his Scottish readers by insisting that the Scots' numbers were very small. He tells us that when the whole force was mustered at Hexham Abbey, they numbered only two thousand men. By contrast, Wyntoun asserts that the English had no less than twenty thousand archers, 'and an abundance of men-at-arms'.

Wyntoun doesn't directly tell us that many of the Scots fled from the battle – he merely mentions that when those who ran away were as many as two miles distant, the battle was still going on. Likewise, he makes no mention of the earl of Douglas's desertion at the height of the battle.

When King David Passed from Home to the Battle of Durham

A thowsand and thre hundyr yhere
And sex and fourty to tha clere,
The Kyng off Frawns set him to ras
And set a sege befor Calays,
And wrate in Scotland till oure Kyng
Specyally be thra praying
To pas on were till Ingland . . .

In the year one thousand three hundred and forty-six, the king of France planned to raise the siege of Calais.

He wrote to Scotland, to our king, begging him to invade England, to make war against one half of the English, so that both halves would be tightly squeezed.

David, our king, was young, strong and jolly, and yearned to see some fighting. He granted the French king's wish, and gathered all his folk together.

He might have been well-contented with his three previous visits to England, to make war against his enemies. Every time, he had managed to return to his own kingdom. Why could he not hold his own land (as it then was) in peace, and keep himself out of danger? He who stands well, should not stir.

But he thought that Fortune had been so kind to his people, giving them victory in dangerous fights, and raising them up to the winning of their own land, that she would continue to stand with them.

But King David did not know, that that is not Fortune's way. Her way is to be forever changing: she would be false to herself if she were to stand still. She should not, therefore, be reproved for being false or treacherous, or for overturning things, since it is in her nature to be forever shifting; winning people's trust with her gifts, great or small, and making fools believe that she will always be generous.

When they trust her and her gifts, that is the moment when she brings them down: and that is what happened to our people, as I shall soon tell you.

What more is to be said? King David quickly gathered his great host, and came to St

Johnstone in the north country, and Ranald of the Isles came to him there. This Ranald was known to be a good man, and had travelled a long way, from his own country, to be with the king during this raid.

The earl of Ross, who was an enemy of Ranald, was also there at the nunnery of Elcho; and Ross made sure he knew exactly where Ranald slept. Ross killed Ranald and seven of his men, then set off home with all his warriors.

The earl, who was worthy and warlike, had brought many warriors with him, and when men knew of this misfortune, they grieved in their hearts, and called it a bad omen. They had only just started out, and such a worthy man had been killed already, and such a large portion of their army gone: this is what they murmured among themselves.

But the king was determined to carry on, despite these losses. He soon passed the Scottish Sea and sped into the marches, where he came to the castle of Liddell. His whole host assembled there. Walter de Selby, who was on the side of the English, was inside the castle.

They besieged that tower with such determination that, at last, they won it, and they slew everyone they found inside, except the women and young children. At that point, William of Douglas, who was wise in the ways of war, advised them to return to their own country. Since they had taken the castle, he said, they could go home without dishonour.

But the other lords who were there said that, whereas his bags were already full, theirs were still empty. They said that they expected to proceed to London, since there were no great men left in England to oppose them: they were all in France, and there were none left but cobblers, skinners and merchants. In short, they did not listen to the Douglas.

They continued their march, and counted their force in Hexham Abbey, where they found that they numbered only two thousand armed men: not enough to take on the might of England.

Soon they passed on to Durham, where they lodged in a park near the city.

They had now been travelling through England for fourteen days, and could get no information about any English force; nevertheless, an English army was assembled in a park nearby. This host consisted of all the most valorous folk north of the Trent, including the archbishop of York, the Lord Percy, the Lord Ferrers, the lords of Rokeby and Lucy, the Lord Neville; and also Copeland and Ogle, among so many others that I cannot list them all here.

They had also assembled twenty thousand archers there, and an abundance of men-at-arms.

The Scots, lying at their park, knew nothing of this assembly, and were occupied with making mirth and enjoying themselves.

Early the next morning, William of Douglas was ordered to make a foray, and he set off in a straight line with most of the Scottish force. These men, who had gone out so early, ran into the English at Ferryhill. There the forayers found themselves in a tight spot: there were too few of them to fight, so they fled. The English rode after them, and martyred five hundred, killing them at Sunderland Bridge. Douglas escaped the chase.

Now the Scottish host was afraid; but nevertheless the worthy men prepared themselves for battle, dividing their army into three echelons. One of these was commanded by the king, another by the Douglas and the earl of Moray. The third, which was by far the biggest, was given to the Stewart.

While they stood in this formation, the English archers came close enough to begin to hit them. Then good Sir John the Graham said to the king, 'Give me a hundred mounted men to go with me, and I will charge those archers and reduce their number: then we will be able to fight more securely.'

This is what he said, but his words had no effect. So he took his horse and rode up on his own, brutally making room among the enemy. When he had ridden like this for awhile, and caused the English to smart, he returned again to the Scots divisions: but his horse was killed.

The earl of Moray and his force were nearby, by some hay-ricks, which broke up their formation, so that they were soon in big trouble.

Those who were still alive sped to the assistance of the king, whose division was trapped in a place that was not advantageous: in fact it was so bad that they could not lift their hands to withstand their foes. From there, some went to help the Stewart's division, which was assembled nearby. There they had more room to stand and fight, and show their quality; but still the Scots divisions were vanquished.

There was hard fighting: men say that such fighting was never seen before. The fighting was so hard that when some of those who ran away were two or three miles distant, many say the standards were still flying, and the face-to-face fighting still continued. But nevertheless, the Scots were soon utterly defeated. Many fled, and never returned; and many were slain.

The king was captured by John of Copeland, who did not hesitate to seize him, though David used a knife to deprive him of two of his teeth.

In the battle, two earls were slain: the earls of Moray and Strathearn, and no less than four earls were taken prisoner: the earls of Fife, Wigtown, Menteith and Sutherland.

They say that five hundred men were killed in the battle, not including those who had been killed during the foray, so that in all, the dead numbered a thousand.

Sir William Douglas was also captured, as was King David.

III. The Cathedral's Point of View

From The Rites of Durham, or A Description or Brief Declaration of All The Ancient Monuments, Rites, & Customs Belonging or Being Within the Monastical Church Of Durham Before The Suppression, Written in 1593. *Published by the Surtees Society, Durham, 1902.*

The corporax cloth, a relic of St Cuthbert mentioned below, would have been a cloth used by Cuthbert when he celebrated mass. Such cloths are also known as corporal or corporas cloths. There are also corporas bags, cases, etc.

The Rites *relates the miraculous story of the appearance of the Black Rood of Scotland, but states that King David II of Scotland, the invader in 1346, was the one who saw the cross tangled in the antlers of a hart. In fact this miraculous experience was vouchsafed to an earlier David, King David I, in 1127. The holy relic is now long lost.*

After the passage below, the author of The Rites of Durham *describes how the rood and St Cuthbert's cloth were sewn into a sumptuous banner that was later taken into battles. The* Rites *continues with detailed descriptions of the stone cross at Neville's Cross, erected to commemorate the battle, and a wooden cross at Maiden's Bower, where Prior Fossor and his monks prayed for an English victory.*

I have broken up the 1902 text into paragraphs, and modernised spelling, typography and some punctuation.

An Ancient Memorial, Collected from the Best Antiquaries Concerning the Battle of Durham, in Prior Fossor's Time

In the night before the Battle of Durham was begun, the 17th day of October, 1346, there appeared to John Fossor, then prior of the abbey of Durham, a vision, commanding him to take the holy corporax cloth, which was within the corporax wherewith St Cuthbert covered the chalice when he used to say mass, and to put the same holy relic upon a spear point, and next morning to repair to a place on the west of the city of Durham, called the Red Hills, and there to remain until the end of the battle.

Which vision the prior taking for a revelation of God's grace and mercy, through the mediation of holy St Cuthbert, went early next morning, with the monks of the said abbey, to the said Red Hills, and there most devoutly prostrated themselves in prayer for victory in the said battle (a great number of Scots pressing by them, with intention to have spoiled them, yet had no power to commit any violence upon such holy persons so occupied in prayer, being protected by the good providence of almighty God, by the mediation of holy St Cuthbert, and the presence of the said holy relic).

And after many conflicts betwixt the English and the Scots, the battle ended, and victory was obtained, to the great overthrow of the Scots: and then the said prior and monks, accompanied with Ralph Lord Neville, and John Neville his son, Lord Percy, and many other worthy nobles of England, returned home, and went to the abbey church, there joining in hearty prayer and thanksgiving to God, and holy St Cuthbert, for the conquest obtained that day.

In which battle a holy cross, taken out of Holyrood House, in Scotland, by King David Bruce, was taken from the said king: which cross is recorded, by most ancient and credible writers, to have come to the said king most miraculously.

Being hunting the wild hart in a forest near Edinburgh, upon Holy Rood Day, commonly called the Exaltation of the Holy Cross, the king separated from his nobles, etc. Suddenly there appeared unto him, as it seemed, a most beautiful hart, running towards him with full speed, which so affrighted his horse, that he violently ran away; but the hart so fiercely and swiftly followed, that he forcibly threw the king and his horse to the ground; who being dismayed, cast back his hands betwixt the tines of the hart's horns to stay himself, when the said cross slipped into his hands most wonderfully; at the sight of which the hart immediately vanished away, and was never after seen, no man knowing certainly what metal or wood the said cross was made of.

In the place where this miracle was so wrought, now springs a fountain, called the Rood Well. The night after the cross so bechanced to him, he was warned in his sleep, by a vision, to build an abbey in the same place; which he diligently observing as a true message from almighty God, sent for workmen into France and Flanders, who, at their arrival were retained, and built the said abbey accordingly, which the king caused to be furnished with regular canons, and dedicated the same in honour of the cross, and placed it most sumptuously in the said abbey, there to remain in a most renowned monument; and so remained, till the king coming to the battle, brought it with him as a miraculous and most fortunate relic.

Notwithstanding that the king, the night before the battle, was in a dream admonished, that in no wise he should attempt to violate the church goods of St Cuthbert, or anything pertaining to that holy saint, which he did most presumptuously disdain, destroying as much as he could of the said goods and lands belonging to St Cuthbert.

He was not only punished by God almighty in his own captivity, being taken in the field of battle, and sore wounded, having first valiantly fought; but there was also taken with him four earls, two lords, the archbishop of St Andrews, one other bishop, one knight, with many others: and in the battle were slain seven earls of Scotland, besides many lords, and fifteen thousand Scotsmen; as also by the loss of the said cross, and many other excellent jewels and monuments which were brought from Scotland, and other noblemen's banners, which were all offered to the shrine of St Cuthbert, for the beautifying and adorning thereof; together with the Black Rood of Scotland (so termed); with Mary and John, made of silver, being as it were smoked all over; which was set up in the pillar next St Cuthbert's shrine, in the south alley.

IV. An English Point of View

From the Chronicle of Lanercost, translation by Herbert Maxwell, 1913.

Lanercost Priory in Cumbria is now a picturesque ruin, open to the public and administered by English Heritage. It was founded late in the twelfth century, and given its northerly location, it was always bound to fall victim to Scottish attacks: this explains the extreme anti-Scottish sentiments expressed in the following account, which is particularly informative on the early days of David II's 1346 invasion of England.

The chronicle covers the years from 1201 to 1346, the year of the Battle of Neville's Cross. It is thought to have been written by Franciscan monks, but somehow ended up in the hands of the Augustinians at Lanercost: towards the end of Lanercost's account of the Battle of Neville's Cross, we learn about an English Franciscan who fought in the battle and did great damage with a cudgel. (Churchmen often fought with cudgels as they were not supposed to draw blood, as they would have been more likely to do with a sword.)

The author of the part of the chronicle printed below is so steeped in Biblical literature that he cannot help comparing, for instance, the Scottish King David with the Old Testament one. He also compares the leaders of the English force with the Maccabees – Jewish rebels who fought the Romans in the second century BC.

Lanercost calls King David of Scotland 'David the defecator' because as a baby he is supposed to have defecated in the font during his baptism.

The version printed below sticks closely to Maxwell's spirited translation, though I have broken up some of Maxwell's paragraphs.

From the Chronicle of Lanercost

In the same year, that is 1346, to wit on the vigil of St Luke the Evangelist, from the root of iniquity in Scotland sprang a stem of evil, from which tree certain branches broke forth, bearing,

I trow, a crop of their own nature; the buds, fruit and foliage of much confusion. For in those days there went forth from Scotland the sons of iniquity, persuading many people by saying, 'Come, let us make an end of the nation of England, so that their name shall no more be had in remembrance!' And the saying seemed good in their eyes.

Wherefore on the sixth day of October, the Scots assembled, children of accursed Belial, to raise war against God's people, to set a sword upon the land, and to ruin peace. David, like another Ahab, deceived by an evil spirit strong men and eager and most ready for war; earls, barons, knights and esquires, with two thousand men-at-arms and twenty thousand commonalty of the villages; who are called 'hobblers' among them, and of foot soldiers and archers it was calculated there were ten thousand and more.

Impelled by pride and led by the devil, these invaded England with a lion-like rush, marching straight upon the fortress of Liddell. Sir William of Douglas arrived with his army at the said fortress in the morning, and David in the evening, laid siege thereto on the aforesaid day.

For three days running they lay there in a circle, nor did they during the said days allow any attacks to be made on the threatened fortress. But on the fourth day, having armed themselves before sunrise with spears, stones, swords and clubs, they delivered assaults from all quarters upon the aforesaid fortress and its defenders. Thus both those within and without the fortress fought fiercely, many being wounded and some slain; until at length some of the Scottish party furnished with beams and house- timbers, earth, stones and fascines [faggots of brushwood], succeeded in filling up the ditches of the fortress.

Then some of the Scots, protected by the shields of men-at-arms, broke through the bottom of the walls with iron tools, and many of them entered the said fortress in this manner without more opposition. Knights and armed men, entering the fortress, killed all whom they found, with few exceptions, and thus obtained full possession of the fortress.

Then Sir Walter de Selby, governor of the fortress, perceiving, alas, that his death was imminent and that there was no possible means of escape for him, besought grace of King David, imploring him repeatedly that, whereas he had to die, he might die as befitted a knight, and that he might end his last day in the field in combat with one of his enemies. But David would not grant this petition either for prayer or price, being long demented with guile, hardened like another Pharaoh, raging, furious, goaded to madness worse than Herod the enemy of the Most High. Then the knight exclaimed, 'O king, greatly to be feared! If thou wouldst have me behold thee acting according to the true kingly manner, I trust yet to receive some drops of grace from the most felicitous fountain of thy bounty.'

O, infamous rage of this wicked king! Alas! he would not even allow the knight to confess, but commanded him to be beheaded instantly; and he had hardly ceased speaking when those limbs of the devil, the tyrant's torturers who were standing by, carried out in act what he had ordered in speech. And thus these evil men, shedders of blood, wickedly and inhumanely caused human blood to flow through the field. Wherefore shortly after God poured forth upon them abundantly his indignation. Thus, therefore, did these wretches, like children, bragging over the fate of a just man, stamp their feet and clap their hands, and they marched forth rejoicing, horse, foot and men-at-arms, David and the devil being their leaders.

Coming then to the priory of Lanercost, where dwell the canons, venerable men and servants of God, they entered arrogantly into the sanctuary, threw out the vessels of the temple, plundered the treasury, shattered the bones, stole the jewels, and destroyed as much as they could.

Thence these sacrilegious men marched by Naworth Castle and the town of Redpath, and so the army arrived in Tynedale. But the English of the Carlisle district had a truce with the Scots at that time, so that in that march they burnt neither towns nor hamlets nor castles within the bounds of Carlisle. David then came to Hexham Priory, where the Black Canons dwell, and, as is to be deplored, on that occasion and on others David utterly despoiled the aforesaid priory; for the Scottish army lay there for three whole days, and David took delight in burning, destroying and wrecking the church of God.

It was, then, not David the warrior, but this David the defecator who, for some reason or other, strictly ordered that four northern towns should not be burnt, to wit, Hexham, Corbridge, Darlington and Durham, because he intended to obtain his victual from them in the winter season; but a certain proverb says, 'The bear wants one way and his leader another.' Wherefore, although the man himself had laid his plans, we were patiently hoping for something different.

The Scots marched from Hexham to the town of Ebchester, ravaging all parts of the country. Thence, praised be God, they crossed toward the wood of Beaurepair for our deliverance and their confusion. David abode in the manor of

Beaurepair, sending forth his satellites in all directions, bidding them drive off cattle, burn houses, kill men and harry the country. In like manner as that other David seized the poor man's lamb, although he himself possessed sheep and oxen as many as he would; wherefore, according to Scripture, his son died; so did this David, a root of iniquity, believing himself like another Antiochus, to possess at least two kingdoms, suddenly attack towns and hamlets, inflict injury upon the people, gather spoil, destroy houses, carry women into captivity, seize men and cattle, and, worst of all, command churches to be burnt and books of law to be thrown into the flames, and thus, alackaday! did he hinder work in the vineyard of the Lord.

He caused, I say, a great slaughter of men, and, uplifted in pride, he declared that he would assuredly see London within a very short time; which purpose the Searcher of Hearts caused to fulfil his fate. Thus this most cruel David was ill at ease, being inspired by the devil and destitute of all kingly grace through his exceeding moroseness.

Who can describe the pride of old men? Scarcely can any one now living reckon up the scourges of the feeble mourners, the groanings of the young people, the weariness of the weepers, the lamentation and wailing of all the humbler folk; for thus the Scripture had been actually fulfilled, 'A voice is heard in Rama, and would not be comforted.'

Goaded by memories sad and joyful I shall not waste time in many words, but pass on briefly to the course of events. Every husband uttered lamentation, and those who were in the bonds of matrimony mourned cheerlessly; young and old, virgins and widows, wailed aloud. It was pitiful to hear. Little children and orphans, crying in the streets, fainted from weeping. Wherefore when the archbishop of York beheld the extreme grief of the people, together with the lamentations of the commonalty, he, like, for instance, that other noble priest, the mourning Mattathias, with his five sons, Abaron and Apphus, Gaddis, Thasi and Maccabeus, did not take to flight like a mercenary, but like a good shepherd went forth against the wolves, with Sir Henry de Percy, Sir John de Mowbray, Sir Rafe de Neville, Sir Henry de Scrope and Sir Thomas de Rokeby, and chose out of the north men prudent and apt for war, in order to deliver his sheep from the fangs of the wolves. He went to Richmond, and lay there several days with his army; but my lord de Percy, with many other valiant men from all parts remained on watch in the country.

The archbishop, then, moved out of Richmond with his army on the day before the ides of October, and directed his march along the straight road to Barnard Castle; and on the morrow he and the other commanders reckoned up their force of men-at-arms, cavalry, foot-soldiers and fighting men upon a certain flat-topped hill, near the aforesaid castle. Also the leaders did there set their army in order of battle, etc., as was proper. They arranged themselves in three columns, whereof Sir Henry de Percy commanded the first, Sir Thomas de Rokeby the second, and the archbishop of York the third – a wise father, chaste and pious, shepherd of his flock.

These men marched cautiously to the town of Auckland, in no spirit of hatred as Cain felt when he slew Abel, nor inflated with any such pride as Absolom's who hung in the tree, putting their trust, not in swords, helmets, lances, corselets, or other gilded armour, but only in the name of Christ, bent upon no invasion but only upon resisting the invaders. Pitching their tents in a certain beautiful woodland near the afore-said town, the English army spent the whole night there.

At dawn next morning, that is on the vigil of St Luke the evangelist, William de Douglas rode forth from the Scottish army with five hundred men to harry the country and gather spoil. Thus the Scots seized their prey in the early morning, but in the evening the English divided the spoil.

On that morning, while the Scots were plundering the town of Merrington, suddenly the weather became inclement, with thick fog. And it came to pass that when they heard the trampling of horses and the shock of armoured men, there fell upon them such a spasm of panic that William and all those with him were utterly at a loss to know which way to turn. Wherefore, as God so willed, they unexpectedly stumbled, to their astonishment, upon the columns of my lord the archbishop of York and Sir Thomas de Rokeby, by whom many of them were killed, but William and two hundred with him who were on armoured horses, escaped for the time, but not without wounds.

Then Robert de Ogle, who is of great strength and not without skill in the art of war, followed them over hill and dale, killing many of the enemy with his own hand, and would not stop until beside a great pool in a certain deep woodland glen his charger, being utterly at a standstill, was quite unable to go further.

Now came William, greatly heated, to the Scottish army, crying aloud with much excitement, 'David! arise quickly; see! all the English have attacked us.' But David declared that could not be so. 'There are no men in England,' said he, 'but wretched monks, lewd priests, swineherds, cobblers and skinners. They dare not face me: I am safe enough.' But they did face him, and, as was afterwards evident, they were feeling his outposts.

'Assuredly,' replied William, 'oh dread king, by thy leave thou wilt find it is otherwise. There are diverse valiant men among them; they are advancing quickly upon us and mean to fight.'

But just before he spoke, two black monks came from Durham to treat with David for a truce. 'See,' said David, 'these false monks are holding conference with me guilefully. For they were detaining me in conclave in order that the English army might attack us while we were thus deceived.'

He ordered them, therefore, to be seized and beheaded at once; but all the Scots were so fully occupied at the time that the monks escaped secretly, serene and scatheless, footing it home without any loss.

On that day David, like another Nebuchadnezzar, caused the fringes of his standard to be made much larger, and declared himself repeatedly to be king of Scots without any hindrance. He ordered his breakfast to be made ready, and said that he would return to it when he had slain the English at the point of the sword. But soon afterwards, yea very soon after, all his servants had to hurry, allowing the food to fall into the fire. Thus David, prince of fools, wished to catch fish in front of the net, and thereby lost many and caught but few. Therefore he failed to carry out the plan he had laid, because, like Aman and Achitophel, that which he had prepared for us befell himself.

So David, having reckoned up his forces, called the Scots to arms — the folk that were eager for war and were about to be scattered; and like Jabin against Joshua, he marshalled three great and strong columns to attack the English. He set Earl Patrick over the first division; but he, like an ignorant fellow, refused to lead the first line, demanding the third, more out of cowardice than eagerness. The Earl of Moray forthwith undertook his (Earl Patrick's) duty, and so held chief command in the first division of the army, and afterwards expired in the battle. With him were many of the valiant men of Scotland, such as the earl of Stratherne, the earl of Fife, John de Douglas (brother of William de Douglas) Sir Alexander de Ramsay, and many other powerful earls and barons, knights and esquires, all of one mind, raging madly with unbridled hatred against the English, pressing forward without pause, relying on their own strength, and, like Satan, bursting with overweening pride, they all thought to reach the stars.

King David himself commanded the second division — not, however, that David of whom they sang in the dance that he had put ten thousand to flight in battle, but that David of whom they declared in public that his stench and ordure had defiled the altar. With him he took the earl of Buchan, Malcolm Fleming, Sir Alexander de Straghern (father and son without the holy spirit), the earl of Menteith, and many others whom we do not know, and whom if we did know, it would be tedious to enumerate.

In the third division was Earl Patrick, who should have been more appropriately named by his countrymen 'Non hic' [not there]. He was late in coming, but he did splendidly, standing all the time afar off, like another Peter; but he would not wait to see the end of the business. In that battle he hurt no man, because he intended to take holy orders and to celebrate mass for the Scots who were killed, knowing how salutary it is to beseech the Lord for the peace of the departed. Nay, at that very time he was a priest, because he led the way in flight for others.

His colleague was Robert Stewart: if one was worth little the other was worth nothing. Overcome by cowardice, he broke his vow to God that he would never await the first blow in battle. He flies with the priest (Earl Patrick) and as a good cleric, will assist the mass to be celebrated by the other. These two, turning their backs, fought with great success, for they entered Scotland with their division and without a single wound; and so they led off the dance, leaving David to dance as he felt inclined.

About the third hour the English army attacked the Scots not far from Durham, the Earl of Angus being in the first division, a noble personage among all those of England, of high courage and remarkable probity, ever ready to fight with spirit for his country, whose good deeds no tongue would suffice to tell.

Sir Henry de Percy, like another Judas Maccabeus, the son of Mattathias, was a fine fighter. This knight, small of stature but sagacious, encouraged all men to take the field by putting himself in the forefront of the battle. Sir Rafe de Neville, an honest and valiant man, bold, wary and greatly to be feared, fought to such effect in the aforesaid battle that, as afterwards appeared, his blows left their marks upon the enemy. Nor was Sir Henry de Scrope behindhand, but had taken his post from the first in the front of the fight, pressing on the enemy.

In command of the second division was my lord the archbishop of York, who, having assembled his men, blessed them all, which devout blessing, by God's grace, took good effect. There was also another bishop of the order of Minorite Friars, who, by way of benediction, commanded the English to fight manfully, always adding that, under the utmost penalty, no man should give quarter to the Scots; and when he attacked the enemy he gave them no indulgence of days from punishment or sin, but severe penance and good absolution with a certain cudgel. He had such power at that time that, with the aforesaid cudgel and without confession of any kind, he absolved the Scots from every lawful act.

In the third division Sir John de Mowbray was abounding in grace and merit. His auspicious renown deserves to be published far and wide with ungrudging praise, for he and all his men behaved in such manner as should earn them honour for all time to come. Sir Thomas de Rokeby, like a noble leader, presented such a cup to the Scots that, once they had tasted it, they had no wish for another draught; and thus he was an example to all beholders of how to fight gallantly for the sacred cause of fatherland. John of Coupland dealt such blows among the enemy that it was said that those who felt the weight of his buffets were not fit to fight any longer.

Then with trumpets blaring, shields clashing, arrows flying, lances thrusting, wounded men yelling and troops shouting, the conflict ended about the hour of vespers, amid sundered armour, broken heads, and, oh how sad! many laid low on the field. The Scots were in full flight, our men slaying them. Praise be to the Most High; victory on that day was with the English. And thus, through the prayers of the blessed Virgin Mary and Saint Cuthbert, confessor of Christ, David and the flower of Scotland fell, by the just award of God, into the pit which they themselves had dug.

This battle, therefore, as aforesaid, was fought between the English and the Scots, wherein but few Englishmen were killed, but nearly the whole of the army of Scotland was either captured or slain. For in that battle fell Robert earl of Moray, Maurice earl of Stratherne, together with the best of the army of Scotland. But David, so-called king of Scotland, was taken prisoner, together with the earls of Fife, of Menteith, and of Wigtown, and Sir William of Douglas and, in addition, a great number of men-at-arms. Not long afterwards, the aforesaid David king of Scots was taken to London with many of the more distinguished captives and confined in prison, the earl of Menteith being there drawn and hanged, quartered, and his limbs sent to various places in England and Scotland. But one of the aforesaid captives, to wit, my lord Malcolm Fleming, earl of Wigtown, was not sent to London by reason of his infirmity, but, grievous to say, was allowed to escape at Bothall through the treachery of his guardian, a certain esquire named Robert de la Vale, and thus returned to Scotland without having to pay ransom.

After the aforesaid battle of Durham, my lord Henry de Percy being ill, my lord of Angus and Ralph de Neville went to Scotland, received Roxburgh Castle on sure terms, patrolled the marches of Scotland, exacting tribute from certain persons beyond the Scottish sea, received others to fealty, and returned to England, not without some losses to their army.

V. From the Chronicle of Jean Froissart, c.1337-1405

The French chronicler seems to have enjoyed the patronage of Edward III's queen, Philippa of Hainault, which may explain why he introduces this lady into the story of the Battle of Neville's Cross, though it is very unlikely that she was really involved. Froissart also tells us that both the bishop of Durham and the archbishop of Canterbury fought in the battle, although Thomas Hatfield, then bishop of Durham, was almost certainly in France at the time, and John de Stratford, the archbishop of Canterbury, would have been in his early seventies.

Froissart also places the battle near Newcastle, not Durham, and he gives a lot of space to John Copeland, who captured the Scottish king and held on to him, despite the orders of the queen. Froissart's imagination may have been tickled by the story of this

humble squire who stumbled upon such wealth,
fame and status.

How the King of Scots, during the siege before Calais, came into England with a great host

It is now a long time since we spoke of King David of Scotland: until now there was no reason to mention him, because the truce was well and truly kept.

But when the king of England was besieging Calais, and lay there before the city, the Scots determined to make war on his country, and to be revenged for the hurts they had suffered before. They said that there were no men of war in the realm of England, because, as they said, they were with the king of England at Calais; or in Brittany, Poitou, or Gascony. The French king did what he could to stir up the Scots to that war, hoping that, if they invaded, the king of England would break up his siege and return home to defend his own realm.

The king of Scots mustered his troops at St John's town on the river Tay in Scotland. Earls, barons, and prelates met him there, and agreed that they should enter into England in all possible haste.

John, Lord of the Isles, who governed the wild Scots, was summoned, because those Scots obeyed him and nobody else: he came with three thousand of the wildest men in all that country.

When all the Scots were assembled, they numbered fifty thousand fighting men. They could not keep their assembly secret enough to stop the queen of England hearing about it: she was then in the marches of the north, near York, and knew all their plans. She summoned many fighting men, and herself stayed at York; after that, all the archers and men of war went to Newcastle with the queen.

Meanwhile, the king of Scots left St John's town and went to Dunfermline. The next day his force passed a little arm of the sea, and so came to Stirling, and then to Edinburgh; there they numbered their company, and found that there were three thousand men of arms, knights and squires, and thirty thousand others on hackneys.

The first English fortress they came to was at Roxburgh. The captain there was Sir William Montacute, and the Scots passed by without any assault, but they went on to burn and destroy the country of Northumberland. Their scouts ran to York, burnt everything outside the walls, and returned to the army, which was within a day's journey of Newcastle-upon-Tyne.

The queen of England, who planned to defend her country, came to Newcastle-upon-Tyne, and waited there for her men: these arrived daily from all over England, and Wales. When the Scots knew that the English were assembled at Newcastle, they approached the city, and their scouts came running before the town. On their return they burnt certain small hamlets thereabouts, so that the smoke came into Newcastle. Some of the Englishmen would have liked to have issued out to fight with them, but their captains would not let them.

The next day the king of Scots, with forty thousand men, came and lodged within three little English miles of Newcastle, in the land of the lord Neville; and the king sent a message to the English in the town, that if they would come out into the field, he would gladly fight with them. The lords and prelates of England said they were content to risk their lives for the right and heritage of their master the king of England: then they all issued out of the town; twelve hundred men at arms, three thousand archers, and seven thousand others, together with the Welshmen.

The Scots came and took their stand nearby, and every man was set in order of battle. The queen rode among her men, and they were arranged into four battalions, one to aid the other. The first division was commanded by the bishop of Durham and the lord Percy; the second by the archbishop of York and the lord Neville; the third by the bishop of Lincoln and the lord Mowbray; the fourth by Lord Edward Balliol, captain of Berwick, the archbishop of Canterbury and the Lord Roos. Every battalion had an equal number of men.

The queen went from battalion to battalion, asking every man to do his duty, to defend the honour of her lord the king of England, and in the name of God, to be of good heart and courage. She promised that she would remember them as well, or better, than if her lord the king were there personally. Then the queen departed from them, recommending them to God and to St George.

Soon the battalions of the Scots began to move forward, and so did the Englishmen: then the archers on both sides began to shoot. The range of the Scots' bows was short, but the archers of England were quick and light, and shot with good aim and skill, and so fiercely that it was terrible to see; so that when the battalions approached each other there was a hard battle.

They began at nine, and carried on till noon: the Scots had great axes, sharp and hard, and gave many hard strokes with them, but finally the English obtained the victory, though they lost many of their men.

Among the Scottish dead were the earls of Fife and Buchan, the earl Patrick, the earls of Sutherland, Strathern and Mar, the earl John Douglas, and the lord Alexander Ramsay, who carried the king's banner; and various other knights and squires.

The king, who had fought valiantly, was badly hurt, and was captured. A squire of Northumberland called John Copeland took him, and as soon as he had the king, he went out of the field with him, with eight of his servants, and rode all that day till he was fifteen leagues from the place of battle.

At night, Copeland came to a castle called Orgulus, and there he said he would not deliver the king of Scots to any man nor woman living, but only to his lord the king of England. On that day the earls of Moray and March, the lords William Douglas and Robert Erskine, the bishops of Aberdeen and St Andrews, and various other knights and barons were also taken captive in the field. Fifteen thousand were slain; and the others saved themselves as well as they could.

This battle was fought near Newcastle, the year of our Lord 1346, the Saturday next after St Michael.

John Copeland put his prisoner in safe keeping in a strong castle, and rode through England till he came to Dover. There he took the sea, and arrived near Calais.

When the king of England saw the squire, he took him by the hand and said, 'Welcome, my squire! By your bravery you have captured my adversary the king of Scots.' The squire knelt down and said, 'Sir, if God by His grace has allowed me to take the king of Scots by true conquest of arms, I think no man ought to envy me; God may send such good fortune to a poor squire, or to a great lord. Sir, I beg you not to be angry with me because I did not deliver the king of Scots to the queen when she asked for him. I hold my rank from you, and I have sworn my oath to you, and not to her.'

The king said, 'John, the good service you have done, and your bravery, is worth so much, that it cancels out your disobedience; shame will follow any who bear you ill-will because of it. You shall return again home to your house, and then I order you to deliver your prisoner to the queen, my wife. As your reward, I will grant you and your heirs five hundred pounds a year in rent, from property you can pick out, near your home. And I hereby make you a squire of my body.'

After three days Copeland departed, and returned to England. When he came home to his own house, he assembled his friends and family together, and they took the king of Scots and rode with him to the city of York. Then, as from the king his lord, Copeland presented the king of Scots to the queen, and excused himself at such length that the queen and her council were content.

Then the queen made good provision for the city of York, the castle of Roxburgh, the city of Durham, the town of Newcastle-upon-Tyne, and all the other garrisons in the marches of Scotland, and left behind the lord Percy and the lord Neville as governors there: then she left York and travelled to London.

The queen set the king of Scots in a strong tower, the Tower of London, with the earl of Moray and all the other prisoners, and set a strong guard over them. Then she went to Dover and took ship, and had such good wind that she arrived near Calais three days before the feast of All Saints. At her coming, the king made a great feast for all the lords and ladies that were there.

The queen had brought many ladies and damsels with her, as her companions, so that they could see their husbands, fathers, brothers and other friends, who were besieging Calais, and had been besieging it for a long time.

Modern English version by SW

Select Bibliography

Burne, Alfred H.: *More Battlefields of England*, Methuen, 1974

Butler, David: *The Battle of Neville's Cross: An Illustrated History,* Durham County Council, 1996

Dickenson, J.W.: *The Battle of Neville's Cross*, Ian Copinger, 1991

Froissart, Jean: *The Chronicles of Froissart*, Macmillan, 1908

Laing, David (ed.): *The Orygynale Cronykil of Scotland by Androw of Wyntoun*, Vol. II, Edmonston and Douglas, 1872

Maxwell, Herbert (trans.): *The Chronicle of Lanercost, 1272-1346*, J. Maclehose, 1913

Oman, Sir Charles: *A History of the Art of War in the Middle Ages Vol. 2: 1278-1485*, Greenhill, 1991

Rollason, David and Prestwich, Michael (eds.): *The Battle of Neville's Cross*, Shaun Tyas, 1998

Sanderson, Patrick (ed.): *The Rites of Durham*, P. Sanderson, 1767

Raine, James (ed.): *Historical Papers and Letters from the Northern Registers*, Longman, 1873

Wadge, Richard: *Arrowstorm: The World of the Archer in the Hundred Years' War*, Spellmount, 2007

For free downloads and more from the Langley Press, visit our website at:

http://tinyurl.com/lpdirect

www.ingramcontent.com/pod-product-compliance
Lightning Source LLC
Chambersburg PA
CBHW021204020426
42331CB00003B/199